CW00432433

EXPECTANT

Jim Cotter
Harlech
26.XI.02

EXPECTANT

Verses for Advent

by

JIM COTTER

CAIRNS PUBLICATIONS
HARLECH
2002

© Jim Cotter 2002

Cairns Publications
Dwylan
Stryd Fawr
Harlech
Gwynedd
LL46 2YA

www.cottercairns.co.uk
office@cottercairns.co.uk

ISBN 1 870652 38 X

Typeset in Enschedé 'Renard'
by Strathmore Publishing Services, London EC1

Printed by Stanley Hunt Ltd, Rushden, Northants.
on Colorit Vanilla Offset

PREFACE

Sing a verse each day of December as you wait for the kettle to boil or the computer to wake up. Find a soloist to sing the verses appropriate to each Sunday of Advent and let the congregation join in the refrain. Or place a soloist in each of four corners of a building. Learn a verse by heart each day and let the image drop from mind to heart to do its own work in your subconscious.

Some of the verses echo the traditional eight Advent antiphons. The tune is the one familiar to those who have sung them. The melody line is provided here. Other verses owe their original inspiration to David Denny and Tessa Bielecki of the Spiritual Life Institute in Colorado, and to Mary Robins. In poetic prose they were first published as *Cries of Advent*, *A Calendar of Meditations*: they are still available from Cairns Publications as a desk-top calendar or as separate cards.

Those familiar with the climax to *The Lord of the Rings* may recognize the eagle of the thirteenth day, and thank you, swallows of Llandecwyn, for teaching me the marvels of your lives and being the inspiration for the eighth day.

JIM COTTER
Harlech, October 2002

COPYRIGHT

VENI, VENI, EMMANUEL

1 the *first* day of December

O come, O come, thou living word,
    and pierce our hearts with healing sword,
    from God's own mouth proceeding far
    to lance the fest'ring wounds of war.
        Rejoice! Rejoice! To mend our strife
        shall come in flesh the God of life.

2 the *second* day of December

O come, O come, thou wisdom strange
from deep within God's womb to range
the earth at midnight's hour of fears
to make us wise beyond our years.
Rejoice! Rejoice! Our God shall leap
with light that rouses us from sleep.

3 the *third* day of December

O come O come, **Adonäi**

in burning bush, on Sinäi,
the flame that holds us still in awe,
to etch in flesh the living law.
Rejoice! Rejoice! **The marks of pain**
shall show the law of love most plain.

4 the *fourth* day of December

O come, O come, thou Jesse's tree,
a lifted sign for all to see,
where words of worldly force shall fail,
and earthly glory's faces pale.
Rejoice! Rejoice! The power of love
through death shall shine in flesh and
blood.

5 the *fifth* day of December

O come, O come, thou David's key,

unlock the gates and set us free.

Descendant of the king of old,

release us from oppression's hold.

Rejoice! Rejoice! In words that sing

true liberty shall soon take wing.

6 the *sixth* day of December

O come, O come, thou living flame
of justice, calling out our name,
in fire our thoughts to clarify,
our wills to sear and purify.
Rejoice! Rejoice! The judge our sore
shall heal, our dignity restore.

7 the *seventh* day of December

O come, O come, thou lion brave,
   and call the cow'ring from their cave,
   course through our veins with thrilling roar,
   inspire with courage, strength, and awe.
      Rejoice! Rejoice! Together we
      the lion, lamb, and child shall see.

8 the *eighth* day of December

O come, O come, thou swallow small,
responding to your infants' call,
fly far and wide across the earth
and end with hope our winter's dearth.
Rejoice! Rejoice! A tiny bird
shall show a truth that seems absurd.

9 the *ninth* day of December

O come, O come, thou cornerstone,
and hold the tensions of your own,
thou keystone of community,
the bearer of humanity.
Rejoice! Rejoice! With arms and face
the crucified shall all embrace.

10 the *tenth* day of December

O come, O come, thou wounded stag,
at home on rugged ridge and crag,
guide us who cut our feet on stone,
and bring us hope, whose bodies groan.
Rejoice! Rejoice! A tender cry
shall smooth our pain and lift us high.

11 the *eleventh* day of December

O come, O come, thou salmon, swift
    to leap the ladder 'gainst our drift,
    to bear our sorrows to the source
    and find in Love the one true force.
        Rejoice! Rejoice! From purest spring
        new life the loving one shall bring.

12 the *twelfth* day of December

O come, O come, thou hidden king
with lightest touch our peace to bring,
with gentle power to reconcile,
and melt away our hate and guile.
Rejoice! Rejoice! The mountain dew
our common clay shall shape anew.

13 the *thirteenth* day of December

O come, O come, thou eagle's eye,
who from an eyrie does espy
a people choking far below
from heat and fumes of lava flow.
Rejoice! Rejoice! The wings shall gyre
to scoop the desp'rate from the fire.

14 the *fourteenth* day of December

O come, O come, thou haunting sound
  that wakes the silenced underground,
  that gives the dungeoned words hard won
  to claim their place beneath the sun.
      Rejoice! Rejoice! The voice enfleshed
      in word and deed shall free
          th'oppressed.

15 the *fifteenth* day of December

O come, O come, thou healing host
around whose table none can boast,
who welcomes home the stigmatized,
their rightful place now realized.
Rejoice! Rejoice! By touching hand
together all in God shall stand.

16 the *sixteenth* day of December

O come, O come, thou morning star,
a point of light so singular,
an unexpected hope so bright
that puts our grey despair to flight.
Rejoice! Rejoice! The radiant dawn
shall soon console the hearts that
mourn.

17 the *seventeenth* day of December

O come, O come, thou lover bold,
    with warm embrace our flesh enfold;
    to love our passion consecrate
    that we with you may new create.
        Rejoice! Rejoice! The chastener
        shall pierce with truth yet melt our fear.

18 the *eighteenth* day of December

O come, O come, appointed one,
      to be God's love for everyone,
      to speak on God's behalf and show
      as much of God as need we know.
          Rejoice! Rejoice! A fragrant oil
          shall soon anoint for blessed toil.

19 the *nineteenth* day of December

O come, O come, Emmanuel,
    God-with-us here and now to dwell,
    at one with our humanity,
    in whom we find our destiny.
        Rejoice! Rejoice! The human face
        of God with us shall interlace.

20 the *twentieth* day of December

O come, O come, thou silent song,
the music of the spheres prolong,
that in our time soon disappears,
yet resonates in list'ning ears.
Rejoice! Rejoice! Through noises shrill
shall clearly sound a voice so still.

21 the *twenty-first* day of December

O come, O come, thou shaft of fire,
to lead us on through dark and mire;
through desert bare thou moving cloud
protect and guide, fulfil what's vowed.
Rejoice! Rejoice! Our God afresh
the covenant shall soon enflesh.

22 the *twenty-second* day of December

O come, O come, thou child of years,
with laughter to allay our fears,
around the cosmos dancing light
to give the demons such a fright.
Rejoice! Rejoice! A girl, a boy,
shall leap into our hearts with joy.

23 the *twenty-third* day of December

O come, O come, thou calling child:

    the creatures, those both tame and wild,

    the weak and pow'rful, coax along

    and change their trembling into song.

        Rejoice! Rejoice! The vuln'rable

        shall make us all insep'rable.

24 the *twenty-fourth* day of December

O come, O come, thou unicorn,
   appearing in our dreams, lovelorn,
   expectant, quiv'ring, innocent,
   wild messenger with God's intent.
      Rejoice! Rejoice! The Spirit shy
      shall come this night with new-born cry.

ABOUT THE FONT 'RENARD'

Renard was designed in 1992 by Fred Smeijers, the renowned Dutch typographer, and issued by the Enschedé Font Foundry. Renard is an interpretation of a 2-line Double Pica Roman (Gros Canon) cut by the Flemisch punchcutter Hendrik van den Keere in around 1570, and shown in Plantin's folio specimen of c.1585. Van den Keere's typeface was cut in a large size for display setting: for use in choirbooks for example. Such a book would be placed in front of the choir, so it had to be legible for all the singers in poor lighting conditions. To achieve legibility the typeface is rather condensed, with a large x-height and dark overall colour. Van den Keere never cut a complete italic, so Renard's italic is a new design, made in the spirit of the period.

ABOUT THE PAPER

This book is printed on 110 gsm Colorit Vanilla Offset from the Stora Mill in Finland, made from pulps from managed sustainable forests, and totally chlorine-free.